First book of saints: their life-st
J 28[...]                                    7

D0122286

Silve[...]

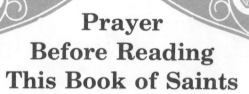

# Prayer
# Before Reading
# This Book of Saints

God our Father,
source of all holiness,
the work of Your hands is clear in your
Saints,
the beauty of Your truth is shown in
their faith.

May I who aspire to have part in their
joy
be filled with the Spirit that blessed
their lives,
so that having shared their faith on
earth
I may also know their peace in Your
Kingdom.

Give me light to understand the beauty
of their teaching and example.
Give me grace to follow them
in their imitation of Your beloved Son.

*Saint Joseph*

# FIRST
# BOOK OF SAINTS

### THEIR LIFE-STORY
### AND EXAMPLE

By
REV. LAWRENCE G. LOVASIK, S.V.D.

CATHOLIC BOOK PUBLISHING COMPANY
NEW YORK

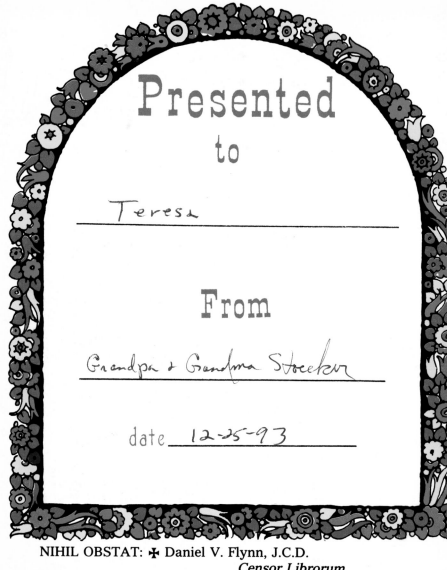

# Presented

## to

Teresa

# From

Grandpa + Grandma Stoecker

date 12-25-93

NIHIL OBSTAT: ✚ Daniel V. Flynn, J.C.D.
*Censor Librorum*

IMPRIMATUR: Joseph T. O'Keefe, D.D.
*Vicar General, Archdiocese of New York*

(T-175)

# FOREWORD

IN the New Testament St. Paul spoke of the Christians as Saints (Colossians 1:2), but early the name was restricted to persons who were eminent for holiness. Saints are persons who distinguished themselves by heroic virtue during life and whom the Church honors as Saints either by her ordinary universal teaching authority or by a solemn definition called canonization.

Canonization implies that the persons are now in heavenly glory, that they may be publicly invoked everywhere, and that their virtues during life or martyr's death are a witness and example to the Catholic faithful.

The Church has abundant doctrine on the meaning of sanctity, its importance for the good of the Church, and the means to become holy. It offers the example and advice of those who in their own lives have reached a high degree of sanctity. The Church says: "Here are models for you to imitate. If you do what they did, according to your ability, and listen to their counsel, you can achieve what they achieved."

This is one of the main reasons for the Church's custom of venerating Saints. They are not only intercessors in heaven but also examples of virtue for the faithful on earth.

May this book on the lives of various Saints help you not only to know them but also to imitate them and to seek their intercession before God.

*Father Lawrence G. Lovasik, S.V.D.*

# CONTENTS

Our Lady Queen of All Saints  5

St. Elizabeth Ann Seton .. 6

St. Agnes .............. 9

St. Francis de Sales ..... 10

St. Thomas Aquinas ...... 13

St. John Bosco .......... 14

St. Bernadette .......... 17

St. Patrick ............. 18

St. John Baptist de la Salle  21

St. Dominic Savio ....... 22

St. Isidore ............. 25

St. Dymphna ............ 27

St. Joan of Arc ......... 28

St. Anthony of Padua .... 31

St. Aloysius Gonzaga ..... 33

St. Thomas More ........ 34

St. John the Baptist ..... 36

St. Maria Goretti ........ 38

St. Benedict ........... 41

St. Kateri Tekakwitha .... 43

St. Anne ............... 45

St. Lawrence ........... 47

St. Clare .............. 48

St. John Berchmans ..... 50

St. Tarcisius ............ 53

St. Bernard ............ 54

St. Pius X .............. 56

St. Rose of Lima ........ 59

St. Augustine ........... 60

St. Peter Claver ......... 63

St. Vincent De Paul ...... 65

St. Therese of the Child Jesus 66

St. Teresa of Avila ...... 69

St. Margaret Mary ....... 70

St. Gerard Majella ....... 73

St. Isaac Jogues ........ 75

St. Stanislaus Kostka .... 77

St. Charles Borromeo .... 78

St. Frances Cabrini ...... 80

St. Elizabeth of Hungary .. 83

St. Cecilia ............. 84

St. Catherine Laboure .... 87

St. Francis Xavier ....... 88

St. Lucy ............... 91

St. John of the Cross .... 93

St. Stephen ........... 95

# Our Lady, Queen of All Saints

**August 22**

AFTER a most holy life and death the Blessed Virgin Mary was gloriously assumed into heaven with soul and body and was crowned Queen of Heaven by her own Son.

All the virtues the Saints practiced are to be found in her in a very wonderful way. She is the Queen of All Saints.

# Saint Elizabeth Ann Seton

January 4

BORN in New York City, August 28, 1774, Elizabeth lost her mother early, and her education became the concern of her father.

At nineteen, Elizabeth married William Magee Seton of New York. Five children were born of their happy union. After her husband's death, the Filicchi—life-long friends—welcomed the grieving widow to their home in Italy.

Elizabeth returned to New York in 1804 and entered the Catholic Church on March 14, 1805. She accepted an invitation from Archbishop Carroll to establish a girls' school in Baltimore. Several women joined her in the religious life, and she became known as "Mother Seton." They were known as Sisters of Charity and lived in Emmitsburg.

A school opened for the children of the parish was the first parochial school in the United States. Elizabeth died on January 4, 1821. In 1963 she became the first American-born citizen to be beatified and on September 14, 1975 she was canonized by Paul VI.

7

# Saint Agnes

A GNES was only twelve years old when she was led to the altar of the pagan goddess Minerva in Rome to offer incense to her. But she raised her hands to Jesus Christ and made the Sign of the Cross.

The soldiers bound her hands and feet. Her young hands were so thin that the chains slipped from her wrists. When the judge saw that she was not afraid of pain, he had her clothes stripped off, and she had to stand in the street before a pagan crowd. She cried out: "Christ will guard His own."

Agnes was offered the hand of a rich young man in marriage, but she answered: "Christ is my Spouse. He chose me first and His I will be. He made my soul beautiful with the jewels of grace and virtue. I belong to Him Whom the angels serve."

She bowed her head to the sword. At one stroke her head was cut off. The name Agnes means "lamb." She was gentle and pure.

# Saint Francis De Sales

FRANCIS was born in a castle in France in 1567. When he was baptized, his mother said: "Now, my son, you are the friend of the angels, the brother of Jesus, the temple of the Holy Spirit, and a member of the Church. Now you must belong to God forever."

Francis received Holy Communion as often as he could. He said: "Jesus is the teacher of holiness. I go to Him because I want Him to teach me how to become a saint. Of what use to me is all I learn in school if I do not become holy?"

Francis became a lawyer, but he was inspired to follow Jesus instead. He wanted to go everywhere to look for the poor and the sinners so that he might win them for Jesus.

Francis became a priest and brought many back to God by his preaching and his kindness. Later he became the bishop of Geneva. He wrote many books and is honored as the patron of spiritual writers. He died in 1622.

# Saint Thomas Aquinas

THOMAS was sent to Naples to study at the Dominican University. After his studies he joined the Dominicans. On his mother's order, Thomas was captured by his brother and kept at home for two years. The Pope called Thomas to Rome to talk to him. He commanded his mother and brothers not to stand in the way of his vocation.

Thomas went back to the Dominicans, who sent him to study in France and Germany. He became a priest and a great teacher. He wrote many books about the teachings of the Catholic Church. Since he was one of the greatest teachers of the Church, he is called Doctor of the Church and Angelic Doctor.

Thomas had a great love for the Blessed Sacrament. While Thomas was praying before a large crucifix, our Lord spoke to him: "Thomas, you have written well of Me. What do you want in return?" Thomas answered: "Lord, I want nothing else but You." He died in the year 1274 at the age of forty-seven. He is the Patron of the Catholic Schools.

# Saint John Bosco

## January 31

JOHN was born on a little farm near Turin, Italy, in 1850. His parents were very poor. He walked four miles every day to school for half the year, and then worked in the fields for a farmer, then a tailor, a baker, a shoemaker, and a carpenter. In this way he worked himself through high school, college, and seminary, and became a priest.

Boys loved Father John. He found places for them to meet, to play, and to pray. He rented an old barn in a field which he called "The Oratory." It was a home for boys, especially the poor boys who needed a home. He started many of these oratories. He believed that prayer and Holy Mass and Communion and confession are the best ways of making boys good.

He was called Don Bosco. He founded the religious order of Salesians, a group of priests who would help him in his work for boys in many countries. They taught boys many trades. Many of the boys became priests. He is known as the Apostle of Youth.

# Saint Bernadette

February 18

BERNADETTE'S parents were very poor. They lived in Lourdes, France.

One day, in 1854, while Bernadette was gathering firewood, a beautiful Lady stood in a cave before her. She was dressed in blue and white, and there was a rose on each of her feet. She smiled at Bernadette and asked her to say the rosary with her.

Bernadette saw the Lady eighteen times. The Lady asked Bernadette to tell the world that people must do penance for their sins and pray. She once told Bernadette: "I do not promise to make you happy in this world, but in heaven."

Large crowds followed Bernadette to the grotto to say the rosary with her. They could not see the Lady. The Lady asked Bernadette to scrape the earth. The miraculous spring of Lourdes started to flow. Many sick people have been cured.

When Bernadette asked the Lady her name, the Lady looked up to heaven and said: "I am the Immaculate Conception." She asked that a chapel be built near the grotto.

Later, Bernadette became a nun and suffered very much, She died at the age of thirty-six.

# Saint Patrick
## March 17

**P**ATRICK was born in Scotland in the year 387. At sixteen he was captured by pirates and sold as a slave to a chief in Ireland. While tending sheep in the mountains, he prayed much.

After six years, a voice from heaven told him to go back to his own country. But first he went to Rome, where he became a priest. He was then sent to England, but after some time he begged the Pope to send him to Ireland. The Pope made him a bishop and then sent him as a missionary to Ireland.

One of the pagan kings of Ireland arrested Patrick. When he saw the miracles worked by Patrick, he said, "Tell us about your God. He has given you great power."

"There is but one God," answered Patrick, "in three Persons: the Father, the Son, the Holy Spirit." Picking up a green shamrock he said, "Even as there are three leaves on this one stem, so there are three Persons in one God." After that he was allowed to preach the new Faith every-where in Ireland. His missionaries later brought the Christian Faith to many parts of Europe.

19

# Saint John Baptist De La Salle

April 7

JOHN La Salle was born in Rheims, France, in 1651. At the age of 11 he began to prepare for the Holy Priesthood and was ordained at 27. He was admired for his great devotion to the Blessed Sacrament.

John was asked to help in two schools in which the teachers were trying to educate their pupils free of charge. He directed the teachers for four years, and then decided to spend his life with them.

John gave away the large fortune his parents had left him. He and the young men then took vows to labor as teachers all their lives, and this was the beginning of the Congregation of the Christian Brothers.

John started a grade and high school and a school where the boys could learn a trade. He also started a school for teachers.

St. John died at Rouen in 1719 and was canonized in 1900. In 1950 Pope Pius XII named him patron of school teachers. He is often called the "father of modern education."

# Saint Dominic Savio

May 6

DOMINIC was born in Riva, Italy, in 1842. When he was five years old, he learned to serve Mass. At twelve he visited St. John Bosco and told him that he wanted to be a priest. They became good friends. Dominic entered the Oratory school, which John Bosco started.

Dominic's shoolmates liked him because he was very kind and cheerful. He studied hard and loved to pray. But his health was poor, and after two years he had to return home.

Dominic always kept these rules, which he had written in a notebook on his First Communion Day: (1) I will go to Confession and to Communion often. (2) I will keep holy the Feastdays. (3) Jesus and Mary will be my best friends. (4) I will rather die than commit a sin.

When Dominic was dying, he said: "What beautiful things I see!" He was only fifteen years old. St. John Bosco wrote the story of his life.

Dominic Savio was made a saint of the Catholic Church and is honored as the patron of teenagers.

23

# Saint Isidore

May 15

ISIDORE was born in Madrid, Spain, in the twelfth century. He was a farmer on the land of a certain wealthy nobleman of Madrid. He never missed daily Mass. The neighbors accused him to his employer of neglecting his work in order to go to Mass, but Isidore said: "I know, Sir, that I am your servant but I have another Master as well, to whom I owe service and obedience."

People tell the story that the employer saw two strangers helping Isidore while he was ploughing. The two men were said to be angels sent by God to share in Isidore's work in return for his attending Mass so faithfully.

Isidore was known for his love for the poor. He brought them food. He also loved animals and took good care of them.

He died on May 15, 1130. The Church honors him as the patron of farmers.

# Saint Dymphna

## May 15

DYMPHNA was born in Ireland in the seventh century. Her father, Damon, a chieftain of great wealth and power, was a pagan. Her mother was a very beautiful and devout Christian.

Dymphna was fourteen when her mother died. Her father was so sad that he sent messengers everywhere to find some women of noble birth like his wife, who would be willing to marry him. When none could be found, his evil advisers told him to marry his own daughter. Dymphna fled from her castle together with a priest, St. Gerebran, and two other friends.

Damon found them in Belgium. He gave orders that the priest's head be cut off. Then he tried to make his daughter return to Ireland with him and to marry him. When she refused, he drew his sword and struck off her head. She was then only fifteen years of age.

St. Dymphna is the patron of those who suffer with mental illness, because her father acted as a man out of his mind when he killed his own daughter.

# Saint Joan of Arc

JOAN was born in France in 1412. She helped her brothers on the farm and often went to a nearby chapel to pray to Jesus.

When she was seventeen, Joan heard the voice of God calling her to drive the enemies of France from the land. Going to the king, whose army was defeated, she asked for a small army. The king believing that God had sent her to save France, gave her a band of brave soldiers.

Joan went before the soldiers carrying her banner with the words: "Jesus, Mary." The soldiers became filled with courage and drove the British army away.

Joan fell into the hands of the British and remained in prison for nine months. She was asked why she had gone to confession almost every day. She said: "My soul can never be made too clean. I firmly believe that I shall surely be saved."

She was taken to the marketplace of Rouen and burned to death. With her eyes on a crucifix, she cried out, "Jesus, Jesus," through the flames.

29

# Saint Anthony of Padua

ANTHONY'S parents were very rich and wanted him to be a great nobleman. But he wanted to be poor for the sake of Jesus, so he became a Franciscan.

Anthony was a great preacher. He was sent out as a missionary in many cities in Italy and France. He brought many sinners back to God through his preaching, prayer, and good example.

One day, when Anthony was praying, the Infant Jesus appeared to him, put His little arms around his neck, and kissed him. this wonderful favor was given to him because he kept his soul from sin and because he loved Jesus very much.

Over and over again God called him to something new in his plan. Each time Anthony answered with zeal to serve his Lord Jesus with all his heart.

Anthony died in a monastery near Padua in 1231 at the age of thirty-six. Many miracles took place after his death. Even today he is called "wonder-worker."

# Saint Aloysius Gonzaga

## June 21

ALOYSIUS lived in the castle of the Gonzaga family in Italy. As a little boy he spent some time with his father in the army. There he picked up rough language. His mother scolded him and taught him what a terrible thing it is to offend God. He began to love prayer and to think about his soul and God.

Aloysius was sent to Madrid, in Spain, to become a page to a prince, and to receive an education. But his motto was: "I was born for greater things." At twenty he signed away forever his right to the lands of the Gonzaga family and became a Jesuit novice.

Aloysius' fellow students loved him because he was kind and willing to help them. They respected him because of his great love for purity.

In Rome Aloysius took care of sick people in a hospital, and before long he himself was ill. The sores caused by the disease were very painful. Aloysius never reached the priesthood; he passed away quietly as he gazed at a crucifix where he found strength to suffer. He was only twenty-three years old. He is a patron of young people.

# Saint Thomas More

June 22

THOMAS More went to school in London. He served as a page for the Archbishop of Canterbury. Later, he studied law.

Thomas married. After the death of his wife, he remarried for the sake of his four children. The family lived happily and shared their money with the poor.

King Henry VIII made him Chancellor of England, a position second only to that of the king himself. Thomas saw that the poor were protected against injustice.

Once while Thomas was at Mass, which he attended every morning, King Henry sent for him. He did not leave until the Mass was finished, but sent this message: "As soon as my audience with the King of Heaven is ended, I will at once obey the desire of my earthly king."

King Henry wanted a law passed making himself head of the Church of England, because the Pope would not grant him a divorce from the Queen. Thomas resigned and was arrested. He suffered much in prison for his Faith. He prayed for the king before he was beheaded in 1535.

# Saint John The Baptist

### June 24

JOHN was the son of the priest Zechariah. His mother was Elizabeth, a cousin of the Blessed Virgin Mary. Mary came to spend three months with her to help her before the birth of John. The Angel Gabriel foretold the birth of John during a vision of Zechariah in the Temple, and told him that John would prepare the people for the coming of the Savior.

When John was a young man he lived in the desert for years. At the River Jordan he cried out: "Do penance, for the kingdom of heaven is at hand! I am the voice of one crying in the desert. Make straight the way of the Lord." Large crowds were baptized by him as a sign of penance and forgiveness of sins.

One day John pointed to Jesus with the words, "Behold the Lamb of God Who takes away the sins of the world!" And when John poured water over the head of Jesus in the Jordan River as a sign of penance, the Holy Spirit appeared in the form of a dove, and the heavenly Father said: "This is My Beloved Son in Whom I am well pleased." King Herod had John beheaded.

# Saint Maria Goretti

MARIA was a beautiful Italian girl of twelve who lived on a farm. One day Alessandro, a nineteen-year-old boy, who was working on the farm, stopped at Maria's house and wanted to do wrong with her.

"No! No!" Maria cried out. "Do not touch me, Alessandro! It is a sin. You will go to hell!"

When Maria began to fight him, he took a knife and stabbed her fourteen times. Maria fell to the floor with a cry of pain: "O God, I am dying! Mamma!" Alessandro ran out of the room.

Maria was taken to the hospital and suffered there for two days. When the priest asked her if she would forgive her murderer, she said: "Yes, I forgive him for the love of Jesus, and I want him to be with me in heaven. May God forgive him!"

Maria died kissing the crucifix and holding a medal of the Blessed Virgin Mary. This happened in 1902.

Maria Goretti was canonized by Pope Pius XII in 1950. She was chosen to be the patron of boys and girls, that she might help them to be pure.

# Saint Benedict

BENEDICT was born in the year 480 in a noble family of Rome. He went to a town called Subiaco, set on a mountain forty miles from Rome. There he lived in a cave in the side of a cliff for three years. Sometimes a raven brought him food.

People heard about this holy man. Soon more than one hundred and forty monks were living with him in a monastery at Subiaco. They were busy every day praying, clearing the land, planting crops, teaching school, feeding the poor. Benedict's motto was: "Pray and work."

Benedict and his monks built a large monastery on Monte Cassino in Italy on the top of a mountain. It became the home of thousands of monks. Later they went out to teach all through Europe. They were called Benedictines. Today they have monasteries all through the world.

Benedict died near the altar where he received the Blessed Sacrament, while his monks held up his arms in prayer.

# Saint Kateri Tekakwitha

## July 14

KATERI was born near the town of Auriesville, New York, in the year 1656, the daughter of a fierce, pagan Mohawk warrior. Jesuit missionaries brought the Catholic Faith to the Mohawk Valley. Kateri was only four years old when her mother died of the disease called small-pox. Her two aunts and uncle adopted her. The disease also disfigured her face.

Kateri was baptized when she was twenty years old. She said she would rather die than give up her Christian Faith. She had much to suffer to be true to her promise.

Kateri went to the new Christian colony of Indians in Canada. Every morning, even in bitterest winter, she stood before the chapel door until it opened at four and remained there until after the last Mass. The Eucharist became her one desire. She was also devoted to Jesus Crucified. She died of a disease on April 17, 1680. Her last words were: "Jesus! Mary! I love you!" when she was twenty four years old. She was known as Kateri of the Mohawks.

# Saint Anne

ANNE was the mother of the Blessed Virgin and the grandmother of Jesus Christ.

She and her husband, Joachim, were very devoted to God. They lived in Nazareth. They had no children, and that was believed to be a punishment of God among the Jews. They prayed to God and begged Him to give them a child. She promised to give her child to God's service.

Their prayers were heard even though Anne was already too old to have children. A daughter was born to Anne, and she called her Miriam or "Mary." Anne offered her child to God at a very early age.

Mary spent some years helping in the Temple. When she returned to Nazareth the Archangel Gabriel appeared to her and told her that she would be the Mother of the Son of God.

St. Anne's name means "grace." God gave her special graces, and the greatest was that she was the mother of the Mother of God. St. Anne is the patron of mothers and of children. Her prayers to Jesus and Mary are very powerful.

46

# Saint Lawrence

August 10

LAWRENCE was the first of the seven deacons who served the Roman Church. His duty was to assist the Pope when celebrating Holy Mass and to give Holy Communion to the people. He was also in charge of the Church property, distributing among the poor the offerings given by the Christians.

When Pope Sixtus was led out to die, Lawrence wept that he, too, could not die along with him. The Pope said: "Do not cry, my son; in three days you will follow me."

Lawrence was arrested. When the governor of the city ordered him to turn over the treasures of the Church, he gathered the poor and the sick. Showing them to the governor, he said: "These are the real treasures of the Church."

According to a popular legend, Lawrence was placed on a gridiron to be roasted over a slow fire. Later he said: "You may turn my body over; it is roasted enough on that side." Lawrence died in the year 258.

# Saint Clare

## August 11

CLARE was the daughter of a count. She heard St. Francis preach in the streets of Assisi and told him of her desire to give herself to God. They became close friends.

Clare refused to marry at 15. At the age of 18 she left her castle with one companion and went to the church of Our Lady of the Angels, where she met Francis and his Brothers. In that poor little church she received a rough woolen habit, exchanged her jeweled belt for a common rope with knots in it, and consecrated her life to God at the altar of Our Lady.

In an old house outside Assisi she started her Order of the Poor Clares. Later, her sister and mother and other noble ladies joined her. They lived a life of prayer, silence, work, and fasting.

One day enemies of the Church were about to attack the convent. The Saint had the Blessed Sacrament placed in a monstrance above the gate of the convent. She prayed for help and the enemy fled. She died in 1253.

# Saint John Berchmans

August 13

JOHN was born in a small town in Belgium in 1599. As a boy John had a very great devotion to Holy Mass and the rosary.

When John was but nine years of age, his mother became ill. As many hours of each day as he could after school he gave to the care of his suffering mother. For three years he was a pupil of a pastor of a parish who prepared boys for the priesthood.

John entered the Jesuit seminary in Rome. There he became ill. He pressed to his heart his crucifix, his rosary, and the book of rules, and said: "These are my three treasures; with these I shall gladly die." He died with his eyes on the crucifix.

In 1888 Pope Leo XIII made him a saint. He is the patron of altar boys, and all boys and girls who want to love Jesus in the Blessed Sacrament and his Mother Mary.

We should pray to St. John for vocations to the Holy Priesthood and the religious life.

52

# Saint Tarcisius

## August 15

TARCISIUS lived in Rome. He served Holy Mass in the catacombs, where the Christians worshiped God because they were persecuted by the pagans.

One day Tarcisius was carrying the Blessed Sacrament to the martyrs in prison when he was caught and beaten. But he did not give up the Eucharist. He died as a boy martyr of the Holy Eucharist. The Christians buried his body with honor in the catacombs. This happened in the third century.

The story of Tarcisius reminds us how much the Christians loved the Blessed Sacrament. Holy Mass and Holy Communion gave them strength to die for their Faith.

Tarcisius teaches children to love Jesus in the Eucharist as their best Friend. He will help them to be good and to make sacrifices for their Holy Faith as Tarcisius did, for he gave his life for the love of Jesus.

We should ask St. Tarcisius for a greater love of Jesus in Holy Communion.

# Saint Bernard

## August 20

BERNARD was born in a castle in Burgundy, France. At an early age he was sent to the best schools. He studied theology and Holy Scripture. After his mother's death, at thé age of 16, he left his home to join a monastery of the Cistercian Order. He became a priest. He was sent with twelve monks to start a new monastery called the Abbey of Clairvaux. Bernard was at once appointed abbot.

The poor and the weak sought Bernard's protection; bishops, kings, and popes asked his advice. Pope Eugenius commanded him to preach a crusade through France and Germany.

Bernard founded many monasteries. Though he was very busy he never allowed himself to forget that his main duty in this world was to lead a holy life and to save his soul.

Bernard is known for his writings and has the title of Doctor of Holy Church. He was devoted to Jesus Crucified and the Virgin Mary. He died in the year 1153.

55

# Saint Pius X

JOSEPH Sarto was the son of a poor village shoemaker and the oldest of eight children. Two priests of the parish helped him.

After ordination Joseph was made an assistant to the pastor in a small Italian town in the mountains. All the people loved him because he was kind. His soul was on fire with the love of God, especially when he preached about the Blessed Sacrament.

When he became Bishop of Mantua, he said: "I shall spare myself neither care nor labor nor earnest prayers for the salvation of souls. My hope is in Christ."

In 1903 Joseph was elected Pope and took the name Pius X. His motto was: "To restore all things in Christ, so that Christ may be all in all." His teaching was: "Love God, and lead good Christian lives." He wanted this goal to come about through frequent Holy Communion, especially early First Communion.

Pius X died on August 20, 1914, with the words: "To restore all things in Christ." He is called the Pope of the Blessed Sacrament."

# Saint Rose of Lima
## August 23

ROSE was born in Peru, South America. She was very obedient to her parents. She did all she was told to do with a happy smile for the love of Jesus. She always tried to help people.

Rose was very beautiful. Her mother wanted her to wear beautiful clothes, but Rose would say: "Mother, only beauty of the soul is important."

A rich young man wanted to marry Rose. He offered her a beautiful home and many servants, but she refused. She loved Jesus with all her heart and wanted to serve God.

When her parents became poor, Rose went out every day to work, and at night did sewing, to help her parents.

Rose visited the homes of the poor and brought them food. She offered all her sufferings and good works to God for sinners. Our Lord often appeared to her as a little child to tell her how pleased he was with her kind deeds.

Rose died when she was only thirty-one years of age. She is the first saint of the Americas.

# Saint Augustine

August 28

AUGUSTINE was born in North Africa in 354. His father was a pagan who wanted his son to be a man of learning, and cared little about his character. His mother was St. Monica, who urged her son to lead a good life.

Augustine fell into bad company and read bad books. For thirteen years he led a very evil life. But his mother kept praying for his conversion. One day while he was reading the letters of St. Paul, he made up his mind to become a Christian. His mother's prayers were answered. Augustine became a Christian at 33, a priest at 36, a bishop at 41. He preached often and wrote many books during thirty-five years as bishop of Hippo in North Africa.

Augustine wrote: "Too late have I loved You, O Beauty of ancient days, yet ever new! Our hearts were made for You, O Lord, and they are restless until they rest in You."

St. Augustine died in the year 430. He is honored as a Doctor or Teacher of the Church, and a patron of theologians.

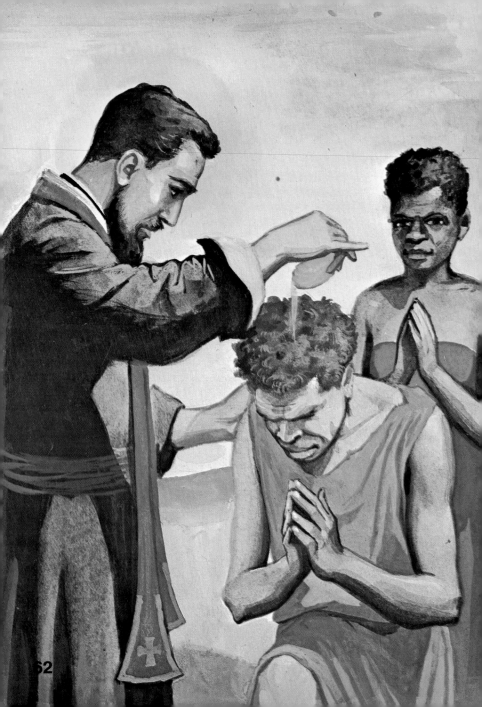

# Saint Peter Claver

September 9

**P**ETER Claver was a Spanish Jesuit. He was sent to Cartagena in South America where he spent forty years in this great slave market of the West Indies, laboring for the salvation of African Black peoples. He called himself "the slave of the slaves." He was their apostle, father, physician, and friend.

When news arrived of a slave ship coming into port, Peter would go on board at once and bring comfort to his dear slaves. He fed and clothed them, and took care of them in their ugly diseases. He baptized forty thousand Black slaves before he went to his reward in 1654.

Peter would say: "We must speak to the Blacks with our hands by giving, before we try to speak to them with our lips." He started charitable societies among the Spanish people to help the slaves.

St. Peter Claver is the patron of the missionary work done among the Black people of the United States.

# Saint Vincent De Paul

VINCENT was born in France in 1576. When he was still a young priest, he was captured by Turkish pirates who sold him into slavery. For two years he had to work hard for the masters who bought him. He converted his last master and was then set free.

Vincent was sent to work in a parish near Paris. He was a very great friend of the poor. He started groups to look after them. The women took care of the sick and cooked meals for them. Men gave food and clothes to the needy.

Vincent started the Order of the Daughters of Charity who worked for the poor and sick. He built homes for the poor, the sick, the aged, and abandoned children. He also started the Congregation of the Mission, a society of priests and missionaries called the Vincentians.

Vincent died in Paris at the age of eighty-four. The St. Vincent de Paul Society continues his work for the poor.

# Saint Therese
# of the Child Jesus

### October 1

WHEN Therese was eight years old she was cured because of the intercession of our Lady.

When Therese was still very young she did kind little deeds for everyone. She prepared for her First Holy Communion by making many little sacrifices. She became a very special friend of Jesus. She once said, "From the age of three, I never refused our good God anything. I have never given him anything but love."

Therese entered the Carmelite convent at the age of fifteen. She wanted to save souls, and to help priests save souls, by prayer, sacrifice, and suffering. Her "Little Way" means loving and trusting in God as a child.

When she was dying, Therese pressed her crucifix to her heart and, looking up to heaven she said: "I love Him! My God, I love You!" She was only twenty-four years old when she died in 1897.

St. Therese is the patroness of the foreign missions.

# Saint Teresa of Avila

October 15

TERESA was the daughter of noble parents in Spain. When she was only seven years of age she and her little brother liked to read stories from the lives of saints. One of their games was playing "hermit" in their father's garden.

When Teresa was still quite young, she became crippled by disease and was unable to walk. She prayed to St. Joseph, who cured her.

Teresa lost her mother when she was twelve. She begged the Mother of God to be her mother. Five years after her mother's death she joined the Carmelite Order. She built many new convents.

By a life of prayer, work, and sacrifice Teresa brought many souls to Jesus. Her many writings show her great love of God. She wrote: "Let nothing trouble you, let nothing make you afraid. All things pass away. God never changes. Patience obtains everything. God alone is enough." She died on October 4, 1582 after she had a vision of Jesus and many saints.

# Saint Margaret Mary

October 16

MARGARET Mary was born in 1647 in France. She was a cripple, but the Blessed Virgin Mary cured her. In thanksgiving she promised to give her life to God. She entered the Order of the Visitation.

Sister Margaret Mary loved our Lord in the Blessed Sacrament very much. He showed her His Sacred Heart in four visions. The flames that came forth from His Sacred Heart were a sign of His burning love for us and His desire that we love Him in return. The crown of thorns around His Heart were a sign of sacrifice and penance to make up for sin.

Jesus said to her: "Look at this Heart which has loved men so much, and yet men do not want to love Me in return. Through you I wish to spread devotion to My Sacred Heart everywhere on earth."

Jesus made at least twelve promises to her. One of these promises is that He would bless those who honor His Sacred Heart and give them the graces they need in life and in death.

71

# Saint Gerard Majella

G ERARD was born in Muro, Italy, in 1726. His father, a tailor, died when the boy was twelve, leaving the family very poor.

Gerard was accepted by the Redemptorists as a lay brother. He served as sacristan, gardener, porter, infirmarian, and tailor.

Even during his life Gerard was called "the wonder-worker" because so many miraculous things happened through his prayers. God gave him special knowledge. He suffered quietly when he was accused of immoral conduct by an evil woman who later confessed her lie. Because he helped a woman who was about to have a child, he is invoked as patron of mothers who are expecting a child.

Gerard died of tuberculosis in 1755 at the age of twenty-nine. He had a small note tacked to his door: "Here the will of God is done, as God wills, and as long as God wills." Brother Gerard was canonized by Pope St. Pius X on December 11, 1904.

# Saint Isaac Jogues

October 19

ISAAC Jogues was born in France in 1607. As a young Jesuit, Isaac, a man of learning, taught literature. He gave up that career to work among the Huron Indians in Canada. He wanted to lead the savage redskins to Christ.

Father Jogues and his companions suffered much and were always in danger of death. On an expedition to Quebec for supplies of medicine and food, Father Jogues and his companions were surrounded by a band of Iroquois. They were taken captives and tortured.

Later, he escaped and returned to France. Several of his fingers had been cut, chewed, or burnt off. Pope Urban VIII gave him permission to offer Mass with his mutilated hands: "It would be shameful that a martyr of Christ be not allowed to drink the blood of Christ."

But his zeal led Father Jogues back to the Huron Indians. He was captured by a Mohawk war party, tomahawked and beheaded in a village near Albany, New York, in 1646. He and his companions were the first martyrs of North America.

# Saint Stanislaus Kostka

November 13

STANISLAUS was born in 1550 of a noble Polish family. At fourteen he studied at the college of the Jesuits in Vienna with his brother Paul. Though Stanislaus was always bright and kind, he was treated badly by his brother for two years. He always forgave his brother.

Stanislaus became very ill. He prayed to St. Barbara to help him. Then he had a vision in which two angels brought Communion to him. The Blessed Virgin Mary cured him and asked him to become a priest in the Society of Jesus. Stanislaus had to leave Vienna because his father did not want him to become a priest.

At Rome Stanislaus lived for ten months as a novice. A priest said to him: "Stanislaus, you love Our Lady very much." "Yes," he replied. "She is my Mother!" And then he said: "The Mother of God is my Mother."

Stanislaus died on the feast of the Assumption of the Blessed Virgin Mary in 1568, at the age of seventeen. His example teaches young people to love Jesus and Mary.

# Saint Charles Borromeo

*November 4*

CHARLES, of the noble family of Borromeo, was born in 1538 in a castle of Aron, in Italy. When Charles was only twenty-two, Pope Pius made him a cardinal and the archbishop of Milan.

Charles was a great teacher and writer. He helped the Church at the time Martin Luther fell away from the Church during the so-called Reformation. His great work was in the Council of Trent. He founded schools for the poor, seminaries for clerics, and through his community of Oblates trained his priests to holiness of life.

Charles also built hospitals where he himself served the sick. He was often seen taking part in public processions with a rope around his neck as a sign of penance. He gave away all he had and wore an old patched cloak. During a great plague, he was ever with the sick and dying. He tried to feed 60,000 poor people everyday.

Charles died at the age of 46 in 1584. He is the patron of seminaries and of those who teach catechism.

# Saint Frances Cabrini

## November 13

FRANCES Cabrini was born in Italy in 1850, one of thirteen children. When she was eighteen years old, poor health kept her from becoming a Sister. She helped her mother and father until their death, and then worked on a farm with her brother and sister.

A priest asked her to teach in a school for girls. She taught for six years. Because a bishop asked her, she started a missionary order in honor of the Sacred Heart of Jesus to care for poor children in schools and hospitals.

Frances wrote to Pope Leo XIII, and he told her: "Go to the United States, my child. There is much work awaiting you there."

She came to the United States with six Sisters in 1889, and began working among the Italian people of New York. She became an American citizen. Mother Cabrini started 67 orphanages, schools, and hospitals in 35 years. She was the first American citizen to become a Saint, July 7, 1946.

# Saint Elizabeth of Hungary

## November 17

ELIZABETH was the daughter of the king of Hungary. At the age of fourteen she was married to Louis of Thuringia, a German prince, and bore three children.

Under the guidance of a Franciscan friar, she led a life of prayer, sacrifice, and service of the poor and sick. Seeking to become one with the poor, she wore simple clothing. Daily she would take bread to hundreds of the poor in the land. They loved her and called her "Dear St. Elizabeth."

One day Elizabeth was carrying bread for the poor. Her husband met her, and looking under the mantle saw only roses.

After her husband's death Elizabeth was left with four children. Giving her money to the poor, she worked to support her family because she was mistreated by her husband's family. She joined the Third Order of St. Francis, spending the remaining few years of her life caring for the poor in a hospital. She died at the age of twenty-four. She is the patron of hospitals.

# Saint Cecilia

November 22

CECILIA is one of the most famous and most loved of the Roman martyrs. According to legend, she was a young Christian of high rank promised in marriage to a Roman named Valerian. Through her example he was converted, and was martyred along with his brother.

An inscription of the fourth century refers to a church named after her, and her feast was celebrated at least in 545. The legend about her death is very beautiful.

Cecilia refused to sacrifice to the gods. The judge condemned her to be smothered by a steam. But God protected her. Then the judge ordered a soldier to kill her with the sword. He struck her three times, but did not cut off her head. She fell down, badly wounded, and for three days she remained alive. After receiving Holy Communion she died in 117. Cecilia is honored as the patroness of religious music. Like any good Christian, she sang in her heart, and sometimes with her voice. She has become a symbol of the Church's teaching that good music is an important part of the liturgy.

85

# Saint Catherine Laboure

CATHERINE was born in 1806 in Burgundy, France, the ninth of eleven children. She refused many offers of marriage, and said: "I found my Bridegroom on the day of my First Communion. To Him alone have I given myself."

Catherine once paid a visit to a hospital which was in the care of the Sisters of Charity. There she saw a picture of St. Vincent de Paul. His example inspired her to take care of the sick and she later shared in the work of St. Vincent de Paul.

The Blessed Virgin Mary appeared to Catherine three times and asked her to spread devotion to her Immaculate Conception. She told Catherine to have a medal made, which is called the Miraculous Medal. On one side of the medal are the words: "O Mary, conceived without sin, pray for us who have recourse to thee," and on the other side the Hearts of Jesus and Mary. This devotion spread throughout the world. Catherine died in 1876.

# Saint Francis Xavier

## December 3

FRANCIS was born in 1506 in Spain of noble parents. He was sent to the College of St. Barbara in Paris and became a teacher. He joined St. Ignatius and four other young men who vowed to work for the conversion of souls. They formed the Society of Jesus.

Before his ordination to the priesthood in Venice, he cared for the sick in a hospital. The King of Portugal wanted six missionaries to preach the Faith in India. One of these was Francis. He journeyed to Goa. There he helped the sick and taught catechism in the church. Later he preached in the south of India and converted thousands of pagans.

Francis sailed for Japan in 1549. Other missionaries joined him there. Thousands were brought to the true Faith. While on a ship going to China, he became very ill of a high fever. The ship stopped at an island. He died there in an old cabin on December 2, 1552.

St. Francis Xavier is the patron of the foreign missions. The flaming heart means his great love for God and for souls.

# Saint Lucy

December 13

LUCY lived in pagan Sicily about the year 300. At an early age she offered herself to God. The rich young man who wanted to marry her was so angry when she refused that he accused her of being a Christian.

Lucy was led to the governor of her city for trial. Unable to make her give up her Faith, he asked: "Is this Holy Spirit in you, this God you speak about?" Lucy answered: "They whose hearts are pure are the temples of the Holy Spirit."

The governor spoke angrily: "But I will make you fall into sin, so that the Holy Spirit will leave you." She replied:"I will never sin, so that the Holy Spirit will give me a greater reward."

Nothing could make her commit sin. She said: "You see now that I am the temple of the Holy Spirit, and that He protects me."

The governor ordered a fire to be lighted around her, but Lucy was not harmed. At last, a sword was buried in her heart. She did not die until a priest came to her with Holy Communion.

# Saint John of the Cross

December 14

JOHN was born in Spain in 1542 of very poor parents. At twenty-one he became a lay brother at a Carmelite monastery, but his superiors sent him to study for the priesthood.

After his ordination he met St. Teresa of Avila, who told him to take up the work of making his own Order more faithful to the teaching and example of Christ. He became the first prior of the Discalced or barefoot Carmelites, and took the name of John of the Cross.

John is a saint because his life was spent according to the words of Jesus: "If anyone wishes to follow Me, let him deny himself and take up his cross daily." Some of his friars cast him into prison. After nine months of suffering he escaped. He wrote: "Live in the world as if only God and your soul were in it; then your heart will never be made captive by any earthly thing."

John died in 1591. Because of his writings on holiness he was declared a Doctor of the Church.

# Saint Stephen

December 26

THE Apostles told the disciples to choose seven men who lived a holy life to help in the care of the poor. These men were called deacons, and Stephen was named first of the deacons. The Apostles ordained them deacons by praying and placing their hands upon them.

Stephen was very holy and brave, and worked great wonders among the people. But some of the Jews accused him of talking against God and Moses. Stephen talked with great wisdom before the court of the Jews. People said there was a halo around his head and his face looked like that of an angel as he spoke bravely of Jesus.

The Jews became very angry. But Stephen being full of the Holy Spirit, looking up to heaven, said: "I see the heavens opened and the Son of Man standing on the right hand of God."

The angry people dragged him outside of the city and stoned him to death. But Stephen forgave his murderers, saying: "Lord, lay not this sin against them. Lord Jesus, receive my spirit." He died as the first martyr.

# Prayer

JESUS, the Church honors the saints
   who are already with You in heaven
because they give us a good example
of the way we should live,
and because they pray to God for us.

Help me to try to love God
with all my heart as the saints did,
and for the love of God to love my neighbor.
But they could not live a holy life
without Your grace.

I ask You to give me the grace
to be more like the saints.

# Other Great Books for Children

**FIRST MASS BOOK**—Ideal Children's Mass Book with all the official Mass prayers. Colored illustrations of the Mass and the Life of Christ. Confession and Communion Prayers.　　Ask for No. 808

**The STORY OF JESUS**—By Father Lovasik, S.V.D. A large-format book with magnificent full colored pictures for young readers to enjoy and learn about the life of Jesus. Each story is told in simple and direct words.　　Ask for No. 535

**CATHOLIC PICTURE BIBLE**—By Rev. L. Lovasik, S.V.D. Thrilling, inspiring and educational for all ages. Over 110 Bible stories retold in simple words, and illustrated in full color.　　Ask for No. 435

**LIVES OF THE SAINTS**—New Revised Edition. Short life of a Saint and prayer for every day of the year. Over 50 illustrations. Ideal for daily meditation and private study.　　Ask for No. 870

**PICTURE BOOK OF SAINTS**—By Rev. L. Lovasik, S.V.D. Illustrated lives of the Saints in full color. It clearly depicts the lives of over 100 popular Saints in word and picture.　　Ask for No. 235

**Saint Joseph CHILDREN'S MISSAL**—This new beautiful Children's Missal, illustrated throughout in full color. Includes official Responses by the people. An ideal gift for First Holy Communion.　　Ask for No. 806

**St. Joseph FIRST CHILDREN'S BIBLE**—By Father Lovasik, S.V.D. Over 50 of the best-loved stories of the Bible retold for children. Each story is written in clear and simple language and illustrated by an attractive and superbly inspiring illustration. A perfect book for introducing very young children to the Bible.　　Ask for No. 135

## WHEREVER CATHOLIC BOOKS ARE SOLD